Young
Martin Luther King, Jr.

"I Have a Dream"

A Troll First-Start® Biography

by Joanne Mattern
illustrated by Allan Eitzen

Troll Associates

Library of Congress Cataloging-in-Publication Data

Mattern, Joanne, (date)
    Young Martin Luther King, Jr.: I have a dream / by Joanne Mattern;
illustrated by Allan Eitzen.
        p.   cm.—(First-start biographies)
    Summary: A simple biography of a great black leader emphasizing
his dream of equal treatment for all Americans.
    ISBN 0-8167-2544-6 (lib. bdg.)   ISBN 0-8167-2545-4 (pbk.)
    1. King, Martin Luther, Jr., 1929-1968—Juvenile literature.
2. Afro-Americans—Biography—Juvenile literature.   3. Civil rights
workers—United States—Biography—Juvenile literature.
4. Baptists—United States—Clergy—Biography—Juvenile literature.
[1. King, Martin Luther, Jr., 1929-1968.   2. Afro-Americans—
Biography.   3. Civil rights workers.] I. Eitzen, Allan, ill.
II. Title.
E185.97.K5M346   1992
323′.092—dc20
[B]   91-26478

Martin Luther King, Jr. was a great American. He led black people in their struggle to win the same rights that white people have.

4

Martin Luther King, Jr. was born in
Atlanta, Georgia on January 15, 1929.
His family called him M.L.

The King family spent a lot of time in church. Reverend King was the pastor of Ebenezer Baptist Church. M.L. loved to sit and listen to his father preach.

M.L. loved sports, too. He and his friends played football, baseball, and basketball. M.L. was one of the best players!

One day when M.L. was 6 years old,
his friends' mother told him he could
not play with her sons anymore.
"We're white and you're colored,"
she said.

M.L. went home, crying. He didn't
understand why the color of his skin
should make a difference to anyone.

M.L.'s mother gave him a hug.
Then she told him a story.

M.L.'s mother told him that at one time, many black people in America were slaves. They had to work hard for white families and do whatever they were told. Now there were no more slaves. But some white people still treated blacks unfairly.

"You are just as good as anyone else,"
M.L.'s mother told him. "And don't
you forget it!"

As Martin grew older, he learned there were many bad laws that treated blacks unfairly.

Black children and white children had
to go to different schools. There were
playgrounds, restaurants, and hotels
where only white people could go.

16

In stores, blacks had to stand in the back and wait until all the white customers had been helped first.

These laws made Martin very sad.
He wanted to do something to change
them. So he studied hard in school.
He read all the time. Sometimes he'd
spend his whole allowance on books.

18

Martin finished high school when
he was only 15. Then he went to
Morehouse College in Atlanta. While
he was there, Martin decided he would
be a minister, just like his father.

Later, Martin went to school in Boston. There he met a pretty girl named Coretta Scott. They fell in love. Soon, she became Mrs. King.

In 1954, Martin got his first job as
a pastor in Montgomery, Alabama.
Something important was about to
happen there.

In 1955, a black woman named Rosa
Parks was riding the bus home after a
long day at work. When the bus driver
told her to give up her seat to a white
man, Mrs. Parks said no. She was
arrested and put in jail.

The black people in Montgomery were very angry. They decided not to ride the buses until the law was changed. Martin helped lead this protest.

For almost a year, black people walked or shared car rides with friends. The bus company lost a lot of money. Finally, the law was changed. Black people could sit wherever they wanted!

After that, Martin led protests all over the South. Many times, people were hurt. Sometimes, Martin was arrested.

No matter what happened, Martin
always said, "Love your enemies." He
would not use violence as a weapon.
He believed in peace.

In 1963, Martin spoke to a huge group
of people in Washington, D.C. "I have
a dream," he told them. He dreamed
that someday *all* Americans would be
treated equally.

In 1964, Martin won a very important
award called the Nobel Peace Prize. It
showed that the whole world admired
his efforts for peace and freedom.

Sadly, not everyone believed in peace. On April 4, 1968, a man killed Martin outside his motel room in Memphis, Tennessee.

Martin Luther King, Jr. had helped to change many unfair laws. And he showed all Americans how important it is to love and respect each other.